MW01170537

A Look at Life

A Book of Poetry

Vol. 1

Belinda Terro Mooney

En Route Books and Media, LLC

Saint Louis, MO

ENROUTE
Make the time

En Route Books and Media, LLC
5705 Rhodes Avenue
St. Louis, MO 63109

Contact us at **contact@enroutebooksandmedia.com**

Cover Credit: Gianna Mooney
Copyright 2024 Belinda Terro Mooney

ISBN-13: 979-8-88870-176-8
Library of Congress Control Number:
2024936890

All rights reserved. No part of this book may be reproduced, stored in a retrieval system, or transmitted in any form, or by any means, electronic, mechanical, photocopying, or otherwise, without the prior written permission of the author.

Dedication

To my wonderful children for whom it was a privilege to teach writing and poetry. I was so honored to watch you develop all your creativity.

Acknowledgments

I am deeply grateful to Gianna Mooney of Angel Break Art for the original cover work. I also want to thank the beta readers from the Catholic Writer's Guild. With praise to God Who gives me everything.

Table of Contents

Dedication i

Acknowledgments iii

Poems and Space for Reader Reflection 1

Life 3

Spiritual Pondering 5

My Destiny 7

On Being the Best I Can Be 9

Dreams 11

Searching for Happiness 13

On Being Beautiful 15

On Being a Child of God 17

My Body is a Temple 19

Can Peace be Bought at Any Price 21

Prayer 23

Detachment 25

Virtues 27

Faith 29

Hope 31

Charity 33
Heart of Love 35
Perseverance 37
Gratitude 39
General Reflections 41

Poems

and Space for Reader Reflection

Reflection

Life

A gift from God,

Our mission strains.

A forward motion

Momentum gains

In order to serve and

Free others from pain.

Reflection

Spiritual Pondering

I wonder at the things God's made.
Creatures, stars, and waterfalls
The trees with restful shade.

I wonder at the things God's made.
Purpose, mission, higher call
God's order and glory arrayed.

Reflection

My Destiny

Heaven is my destiny.
It calls, it waits for me.
Heaven is my destiny.
There God I long to see.

Heaven is my destiny.
His Face I shall behold.
Heaven is my destiny.
Happiness untold.

Reflection

On Being the Best I Can Be

I decided as a little child
To be my very best
My best self at all times
Is my motto and my crest.

Reflection

Dreams

Great expectation, humble desires,

Things longed for and courted.

Some new, some tried.

Dreams endure in the human spirit.

Aspirations once born never die.

Reflection

Searching for Happiness

Happiness when sought without
Can only end in pain.
But happiness when sought within,
With God is always gain.
So, seek your happiness within
Achieve your heart's desire
And find your peace again.

Reflection

On Being Beautiful

Beauty is akin to goodness—
With truth, it goes hand in hand.
People striving for true beauty
Cooperate with God's plan.

Reflection

On Being a Child of God

I never did deserve this gift:

I certainly received it

Adoption as a child of God

Light for the world now lit.

Reflection

My Body is a Temple

My body is a temple
Of the God who dwells within—
The God who made it beautiful
Maintains it strong, and then
Renews my life, refreshes me
And leads me on to Him.

Reflection

Can Peace be Bought at Any Price

Can peace be bought at any price?
Can character be compromised?
I think that price is much too high.
Integrity is to be prized.

Reflection

Prayer

God descends, comes close to us,

Whispers love and hope.

We rest, listen, and speak

Receive direction and His peace.

Reflection

Detachment

Mind my own business
I am wont to say
As I get busy with
My own work today.

Live and let live
Is my motto of how
I will put my affairs
In order right now.

Reflection

Virtues

To be the best that we can be

Takes virtue and magnanimity.

Patience, diligence, and perseverance too.

To attain the goal, this we must pursue.

Reflection

Faith

Believing and trusting in Someone unseen,
Knowing that He is guiding, taking
The solid assurance that Power's at hand
Will keep our souls in the virtue of faith.

Reflection

Hope

An understanding that all will be well;

Gratitude for what is now known,

The thoughtful expectation of what is beyond

Will keep our souls in the virtue of hope.

Reflection

Charity

Patience and kindness, mercy toward others
Steadfast belief in their goodness with clarity,
Accepting, affirming, assisting generously
Will keep our souls in the virtue of charity.

Reflection

Heart of Love

A baby cries
His mother hears;
It seems her heart
Has special ears.

Attend to need,
Give comfort too—
A hug, a kiss,
The tears are soothed.

Reflection

Perseverance

Perseverance takes work to get yourself going

In mind first, then in body as well

To focus, to stick to the task at hand,

To finish the project according to plan.

Reflection

Gratitude

A sunlit day with clouds afloat
A tranquil spirit that all surveys
The trees, the houses, the people—
It basks in God's ways.

A sunlit day with clouds afloat
A tranquil spirit that all surveys
The memories of a well-lived life,
Of love and hope and length of days.

General Reflections

Made in the USA
Columbia, SC
07 September 2024

828aa5af-034c-4252-ad4a-2ec4a949d3bbR01